SLOW
TWITCH

A Collection of Poems

Essie
Sappenfield

Slow Twitch

by Essie Sappenfield

Essie Sappenfield

Nashville, Tennessee

ISBN: 979-8-218-78054-8 (Paperback)

ISBN: 979-8-218-52859-1 (E-book)

First Edition: September 2025

TABLE OF CONTENTS

I.
SLOW TWITCH

CLEMENCIES

I go down the street in my gown and robe
to get George to play with Alexei.
Being an old coot, they cut me some slack.
Besides, it's a collaborative neighborhood;
I know where to find my cumin and my corkscrew.

This is one of those November days
when nature says to hell with the calendar
and trots out one more perfect reprieve.
Shards of color cling to the trees.

Alexei's elegant body dances to greet us
when we come into the yard. I see
they've picked up the garbage. I drag the can
down the flagstones. One day
I won't be able to do this. My azaleas
aren't scared of winter. My doomed lantana
blooms its little heart out.
How can I stand such beauty?
How can I hold such happiness?

I go inside to take my pills, do my stretches,
plan what to eat,
a mulching,
a prayer
that I might winter over.

SEE YOU STIFFEN

I see you stiffen
when I say "let's talk"– aged
shoe waiting to drop.

EAVESDROPPING IN A K-15 DINER

"She used to really get after me,
then she'd send me home with a Care package.
You know, she made those rolls.
I'd ration them out,
give one to Mama and one to Sister
and keep the rest for myself.
She made candied apples, too.
I could get ahold of those apples
and those rolls—
I'd just forget about everything.

"That was one of the best things
My mother's brother ever did,
was marry her.
I'd see her throw in a pinch of this
and a pinch of that
and come up with the best cooking. Once
I saw him threaten her with a gun.
She made fried pies, too.
You know what they are.
They've got filling in the middle,
and then you fold over the dough
and mash it down on the sides.
Me, I have to follow a recipe."

HOW TO BE REAL

Show up, screw up, 'fess
up. Repeat. The future you
will thank you, darlin'.

CHRISTMAS GREETING POST PANDEMIC

In spite of fatigue and financial excess
the coming of Christmas persists to suggest
neither failures past,
nor flubs yet to come,
nor fame, nor flame,
nor fear, nor flood,
nor famine, nor flu,
nor fetish, nor fiend,
nor fools, nor fake news, nor bad air, nor bad hair,
nor the feckless cruel who fuel despair,
can cleave us from the source
that torques the whole
and flings the stars
and sparks the zeal
of fungi and flora
and caged cockatiel
to grow,
to thrive,
evolve,
survive.

THUS, SPAKE LEE TUCKER, QUOTING SOMEONE SOMEWHERE

I'm not much,
   but I am
all I think about.

ASPIRATIONS

This poem is for you, my daughter,
who grew up underwater. Your father
found the light kinder there. We swam
in the beauty of filtered sunlight
and kelp. Our lamprey mouths
sucked breath where we could find it,
and you, inexhaustible as the sea.

One day you found a dead bird
The wonder part has gone out of him, I said.
My wonder part is in my feet, you said.
Heedlessly, we watched as seaweed bound them.

One day you stood on the stage.
Your hand shook.
The bow screeched.
Your suffocation exposed,
bare as a bone,
shattered my denial.

Then the undertow, and he was gone.
We climbed ashore, you on one bank,
I on another, dragging sea slime
and filling our lungs.

Now we live as separate species.
Too late I would save you.
We meet for lunch, for coffee,
mindful not to mention remnants
of our past, evidence of the time
when once we breathed
and bullied each other
and licked the wounds of affection.

THAT TIME WE TOUCHED

From a primal pose
two rose as One with healing
sprouting in Her wings.

HOW TO GET OUT OF BED

push the snooze
button   push
it again   and again   enjoy
your bubble-up thoughts
when they pull you under
decide to save yourself
make a list: three things
I must do three
    I want to do
        three I should
do   remember: you eat
an elephant one bite at a time
    it's not about the elephant

who will love me
what was I born to do
why can't I get
out of bed   picture yourself
on the streets
the guilt starts
why aren't I grateful
say fuck it   say help me
remember that chihuahua
in your brain   yips
bad girl   bad girl
just because
it can   say I've come
so far   does anyone care

don't go there
remember
it's all holy
this wrinkled hand
this lethargy
this hiding
you laugh   you sit up
you are just another living creature
sniff the day

OVERHEARD AT GARZA LITTLE ELM RESERVOIR

"Saw this newbie sailing in circles,
so we sail over to him.
The closer we get, the more he slumps down,
till he lies below the rim.

"We look over the gunnels and see him,
Pinned, like a specimen.
'Do you need any help?' Poor shmuck shakes his head."
I've lived my life that way, too.

THUS, SPAKE GEORGE GRIGG

"It'll be alright.
We may have to change our minds
about what that means."

VILLANELLE

In the nightclub of my heart, two partners wait.
One sashays hope; one slogs despair.
Which one to choose should not require debate,

Unless I find myself in such a state that choosing
hope is more than I can dare.
On the dance floor of my heart two partners wait.

Sometimes I'm tired, and I capitulate.
Hope is hard work, takes more time to prepare,
Put on my shoes, warm up, forgo debate.

Despair's an always-disappointing date.
With hope I feel I'm dancing with Astaire.
In the night club of my heart two partners wait.

I find I cannot dance as fast of late—
fewer steps, but with more savoir-faire.
And if my feeble tango should abate,

I'll throw my head back and I'll ululate
for joy—for hope is now my go-to prayer.
On the dance floor of my heart two partners wait,
And I no longer can afford debate.

THUS, SPAKE UNCLE PHIN

To his brown-eyed niece,
"The moment you care about
something, they've got you."

LESSON

Aunt Mattie took the train from Cooke County
to San Marcos to the teacher's college,
in case she didn't marry.   She met a man
not cut out to be a teacher.
They planned to marry.   Her parents
wouldn't have it.   She taught school.
Then Uncle Horace, gentle, local, farmer,
older, less exciting, proposed.   Him,
they approved.   My mother
remembered: Granny hemming
Aunt Mattie's wedding dress and Aunt Mattie
stamping her foot, and saying, "Next time
I'll marry who *I* want to marry."
They tried to protect her
from the school of hard knocks.
Even soft knocks can teach you
the next test will not be the one you studied for.

THUS, SPAKE CAROL FREEMAN

"Just do the little
bit you can do," she told me.
"It will turn out right."

TEEL

A starless night.
Ellington's on the square,
Confederate soldier standing guard.
We'd each had our traumas.
Your son had died of AIDS.
No nurse would touch him
or care for him.
You told how you had held him dying
in your arms and kissed him on the lips.
That vision became my Pietà.
I remembered the Madonnas on your mantle.

After 30 years in Denton, I was fixing to move, to try
marriage just one more time.
You gave me a poster with shoes and my name
spelled all whichaways.
"Travelling Shoes for Essie."
When I agonized whether I was doing the right thing
you reached across the table
and cradled my hand.

"Essie," you said, "It will never again
be as bad as it once was."

MAKING (OR NOT) THE BED

I did not make my bed today.
It seemed a futile act.
How could such a meager deed
Make up for all I lack?

I went back this afternoon
To start my day anew,
Feeling blessed to cherish
The lesser I can do.

IN ALL THINGS

To see grace in a root canal –
Those of us who run from pain –
Takes a sharp and eager eye
A willing, nimble brain.

A grain of sand sometimes provokes
A pearl made by the mother.
Life is – unless I press Reset–
One irritation after another.

CONUNDRUM

Dreary morning.   Still
in bed.   Hungry.   The kitchen
is a long way off.

JOURNEY MERCIES

I've got miles on me you can tell by looking,
And Celeste, her odometer reads
one hundred ninety-five thousand
three hundred and two.
Two faithful hags heading home to the barn.

This road, this lonely stretch of K-15
wears hard on us,
black skunks shocked
with white rolled up like plush toys,
and on the shoulder grit
a smear with a possom's naked tail.

Last month Celeste caught a deer—
a fawn no bigger than a dog—
still shags a clutch of hair
on her right front bumper.

But today, wild roses clamor
up a barbed wire fence,
in the bar ditch a red wing
blackbird sings from a cattail,
and just this side of Mulvane
a line of cars bumps out
around a box turtle
creeping toward Udall.

ADAPTATION

Sleepless nights alone –
a man – a dog – or this time
I might learn to pray –

YOUR LOSSES LIVE WITH YOU

Your losses live with you,
Like troubled teens,
Because no one else will take them.
The easy conversations,
The woman who chased the cat
Then never came back,
The friend who pestered you
And made you laugh,
You found on her kitchen floor,
Her long blond hair
Spread out like a halo.

Unruly brats!
You want to chain them up
In the basement
So you can move on.
Good luck with that.
They will pound the pipes
And thump the floor
Until you learn you have
Nowhere else to go.

Grow up.
Throw open your arms
And hug them close.
Wipe their tears.
Give them your best beds.
And when they come out
To talk, give them the seat of honor.

See what they want to drink.
Pull up your chair.
The conversations will be harder now,
But the pain feeds you.
You know your story.

DEVILLED EGGS

Put your last ten eggs in a pan and cover with water.
Forget about them.
After a few hours discover them on the stove.
Say, "I'd better cook those."
Turn burner to high.
Forget about them.
Answer emails.
When you hear a sound like rain on the roof,
look out the back door.
It's dry.
Think: it must be my upstairs neighbors.
Forget about it.
Play Spider Solitaire.
When you hear a sound like rain on the roof,
look out the kitchen windows.
Remember the eggs.
Douse them with cold water in the sink.
Drain.
Douse again.
Put two handfuls of ice into the pan.
Crack one egg and shuck it.
Cut it in half. It looks done.
Eat one half just to make sure.
Dip them in ice water as you peel them.
They come out slick and smooth as a baby's bottom.
Now study the remaining half of the first egg, a per-
fect circle inside a perfect oval.
It's said the cosmic egg hatched the world.
   From the yolk the sun was made,
   From the white the moon.
You hold, in your hand, an artifact
from our long search for meaning. Eat it.

Now you have nine perfect eggs, square of the sacred three.
Cut them in half, fill with your gratitude, your longings,
the lore of all the cooks who went before.
Set them out to feed the soul,
as only devilled eggs can.

SLOW TWITCH

Hope is a slow twitch
muscle, built not with quick reps,
but steady holding.

THUS, SPAKE MISS ETHYL

That October she
was eighty, telling us, "Stay
awake and fear not."

HAZEL

I don't do Facebook.
I've never been good at keeping up
with people once I leave.
Forty years after it happened,
after both parents were dead,
I went home to ask neighbors
what they remembered about the time
my father lost his job.
The street was much the same, the houses
shabbier, the mesquite trees,
the vacant lot where we dug fox holes
before I had to be a good girl and make
the family proud, before the firing
that neither parent, shamed, would talk about.
Surely it was not just "politics," like Mama said.
Somehow, I was to blame.

Married and abandoned when her husband
learned she had MS, Hazel moved back
to the house she grew up in. Along with her own
tragic history, she carried too, the memory of
what her parents had said.
"The worst thing that ever happened
to the Donna schools," she reported.
"A terrible hurt to your family."
I remembered the English teacher had died,
and the history teacher retired. He wanted
to hire new teachers. The Superintendent thought
the coaches could do those jobs.

She knew no hidden secret, no scandal.
behind the shame I'd carried all those years.

Only admiration. "Just politics,"
my mother said then.
Just an ordinary tragedy in a small Texas town.
Hazel gave me a precious gift,
asking in return only a photograph
of my family as it was then.
I did look, a little.
I've never been good at follow through.

WHY DID IT TAKE SO LONG TO LEARN

To clean house without feeling my mother had won?
To drive to work without fearing bag ladies?
To send flowers without fighting my father's "tentacles of
        capitalism?"
To go to bed without hearing prowlers?
To dress without hearing a fashion critique?
To hear Renee Fleming without feeling I'd wasted my life?
To travel without thinking, "What I shoulda done . . ."?
To walk my dog without competing?
To listen without waiting to pounce?
To say "I'm sorry" without shame?
To look in the mirror and smile at the woman
       who is doing her damnedest
       without minding that God is winning?
That these life hacks would be the work of a lifetime?

EVEN IN EERIE, EGREGIOUS TIMES

Even in eerie
egregious times, life carneys
peepshows of delight –

Tiny trilliums
bloom. Mockingbirds sing a wing
span from the spook house –

BY THE TIME THE JURY
COMES IN

By the time the jury comes in on how you turned out,
no court has jurisdiction, if you live long enough.
Skewered as I was by the Parable of the Talents,
I see myself roasting on a spit in hell.
And in the Night Tribunal I writhe: the boats
that sailed without me, the student I swindled,
the child abused because I looked the other way.
Old mentors shake their heads.
They'd expected better.

Awake, I stretch and sigh. Battle fatigue.
Sixty years in the trenches takes its toll.
I come up for air, feed the cat, call a friend. We laugh
about parts that don't work and words we can't recall.
Outside, a rumpled cardinal hunkers on a pine branch
whose icy needles sparkle in the sun like tensile.

I've given up hope of mounting a defense.
But I would like to meet the One Who Remembers
to show how mercy rides the ripples of happenstance.
And then, because you cannot look on God and live,
I'd be incinerated on the spot,
caught up in the next inhalation,
and breathed out to nourish a new creation.

OLD FRIENDS

Four of us, giddy
to be together, hobble
out to see the stars.

II.
PLEAS

INTRODUCTION TO PLEAS SECTION

Esther De Waal in England and Rabbi Rami Shapiro in Nashville introduced me to the idea that I could enrich my life by turning chores into rituals and blessing difficult situations. De Waal has written several books on Celtic Christianity. I found her book "The Celtic Way of Prayer" especially helpful. Rabbi Rami Shapiro has written many books and given workshops, where he taught us Hebrew prayers for daily tasks. These pleas are mine.

MAKING THE BED

I make my bed and thank You
for bringing me safely through the night.
I smooth this sheet as a prayer that You
will calm me, bless me and order my life.

I OPEN MY EYES

I open my eyes on a gray day.
Wrap Your love around me.
Hold my hand as I walk through the clutter
of my hopes and fears
and dying dreams.

FEAR

I lie, pinned to my bed.
Fear coils itself around my heart.
The flies of failure buzz.
You, who raised Lazarus,
take my hand.

BRUSHING MY TEETH

I brush my teeth.
May my every breath speak
of rightness and truth
and more than a hint of grace.

ON THE TOILET

Some Jews have a prayer for this,
reminding us to let go
of what we do not need
so we may love You better.
I am fearfully and wonderfully made.
Thank you that so many of my parts
work so well.
Help me love all Your creation,
even this.

FOR DRESSING

I clothe myself in rightness and joy
as a soldier dresses for battle.
Let this shirt come between me and harm.
Let these shoes find the path to You.
Let these earrings sparkle
as sunlight on water
and dance me to the heart of wonder.

OPENING THE MAIL

I open my mail to see
what You have sent me.
Bless the friends who remember me.
Shield me from the waste
of wanting what I do not need.
Be my hand as I winnow the post.

BE MY PEN

Be my pen as I write these words.
Be the paper that receives them.
Let no triteness come
between me and Thee.

I WASH THIS PLATE

I wash this plate in soapy water.
My cloth circles three times
for the sacred trinity,
the eternal order of three,
whose Name is far beyond my knowing.

FLYING

I board this plane
and put myself into Your hands.
Bear us up on the wings of love.
Be the eyes and the hands
of those who fly this plane.
Be the hearts of this company of travelers.
Let us know the kindness of encounter.
Let us care for one another.

MORNING PRAYER

Our Mother who births the world,
Your sacred name is my own.
Let me see with Your eyes,
Let me hear with Your ears,
Let Your will be my heart's desire.
Give me today what I need,
And teach me to forgive,
Just as You are always forgiving me.
Wrap your wings around me
And hold me close to Your beating heart,
For it is You who is good,
It is You who is wise,
It is You who remains
When my world falls away.

ACKNOWLEDGEMENTS

I am indebted to many friends and poets, singly or in writers' groups, who have read and listened, encouraged me over the years and given me permission to use their words.

I have been greatly helped by Virginia Owens, Naomi Hirahara, The Milton Center, The Porch, Ciona Rouse, John Jenkinson, Emilia Amos, Rick Sale and Janet Peery. Thanks to Angie Li for her help with technical logistics and cover art.

I would also thank Carlin Sappenfield, Fiona Sappenfield, Sophia Ellingham, Foster Brooks, Rita Blanchard, Sue Farley, Susan Johnston, and my friends in Germantown Commons Cohousing Community.

In this book of new and collected poems, Essie gathers the best of her work. She has published in *Calyx*, *Kalliope*, *13th Moon*, *Winfield (KS) Daily Courier*, *The Wichita Eagle*, and *QuartetJournal* online.

Essie grew up in Texas when people talked in colorful idioms and quoted the King James Bible. Those cadences, along with her penchant for eavesdropping, give her poems a conversational style. She lives in Germantown Commons cohousing community, Nashville, Tennessee.

"Through metaphor and life experience, Sappenfield celebrates the good as well as the bad bumps in the road."

—Jane C. Miller,
co-editor Quartet Journal

She writes good poems. Read 'em.
—Virginia Stem Owens